CHOCOLATE CHIP
COOKIES

by Candice Ransom

Cody Koala

An Imprint of Pop!

popbooksonline.com

abdobooks.com

Published by Pop!, a division of ABDO, PO Box 398166, Minneapolis, Minnesota 55439. Copyright © 2019 by POP, LLC. International copyrights reserved in all countries. No part of this book may be reproduced in any form without written permission from the publisher. Pop!™ is a trademark and logo of POP, LLC.

Printed in the United States of America, North Mankato, Minnesota

082018
012019

THIS BOOK CONTAINS
RECYCLED MATERIALS

Cover Photo: Shutterstock Images
Interior Photos: Shutterstock Images, 1, 6–7, 10, 15, 16, 19 (top), 19 (bottom left), 19 (bottom right); INTERFOTO/Alamy, 5 (top); Chronicle/Alamy, 5 (bottom left), 5 (bottom right); iStockphoto, 9, 13, 21

Editor: Charly Haley
Series Designer: Laura Mitchell

Library of Congress Control Number: 2018949237
Publisher's Cataloging-in-Publication Data

Names: Ransom, Candice, author.
Title: Chocolate chip cookies / by Candice Ransom.
Description: Minneapolis, Minnesota: Pop!, 2019 | Series: Favorite foods | Includes online resources and index.
Identifiers: ISBN 9781532161872 (lib. bdg.) | ISBN 9781641855587 (pbk) | ISBN 9781532162930 (ebook)
Subjects: LCSH: Chocolate chip cookies--Juvenile literature. | Foods--Juvenile literature. | Children's eating habits--Juvenile literature. | Food preferences--Juvenile literature.
Classification: DDC 641--dc23

Hello! My name is

Cody Koala

Pop open this book and you'll find QR codes like this one, loaded with information, so you can learn even more!

Scan this code* and others like it while you read, or visit the website below to make this book pop.

popbooksonline.com/chocolate-chip-cookies

*Scanning QR codes requires a web-enabled smart device with a QR code reader app and a camera.

Table of Contents

Chapter 1

Cookies and Ice Cream

Ruth Wakefield opened the Toll House Inn restaurant in 1930. It was on a busy highway in Massachusetts. A thousand people ate there each day.

Watch a video here!

Everyone liked ice cream with butterscotch nut cookies. Wakefield decided to bake a brand-new cookie.

People in **ancient** Egypt made cookies with honey. Cookies came to America in the 1600s.

Chapter 2

New Cookie

Wakefield mixed flour, brown sugar, and eggs in a bowl. Then she picked up a bar of chocolate. She added chunks of chocolate to the cookie **dough**.

Learn more here!

The cookies turned out crispy with chocolate bumps. Wakefield called them Toll House Chocolate Crunch Cookies.

Chocolate comes from the beans of **cacao** trees.

Chapter 3

Favorite Cookie

Wakefield's cookies became famous. She talked about them on a radio show. Her **recipe** was printed in newspapers.

Learn more here!

A chocolate bar company sold bits of chocolate in bags. Wakefield's cookie recipe was on the back of the bag.

Toll House cookie dough is sold in stores today.

The company gave
Wakefield free chocolate
chips for the rest of her life!

Today there are many types of chocolate chip cookies. People have changed Wakefield's recipe to make it their own.

Chapter 4

How to Bake Cookies

Have an adult set the oven to 375 degrees. Read the recipe on the chocolate chip bag. Measure the **ingredients**. Stir the ingredients together to make the dough.

Complete an activity here!

Scoop out dough with a spoon. Place dough balls on the cookie pan. Bake them for 9 to 12 minutes. They should turn light brown. Let the cookies cool before eating.

Chocolate Chip Cookie Ingredients

- all-purpose flour
- brown sugar
- white sugar
- baking soda
- vanilla extract

- salt
- eggs
- butter
- chocolate chips

Making Connections

Text-to-Self

Do you like to eat chocolate chip cookies? What is your favorite food?

Text-to-Text

Have you read any other books about food? What did you learn?

Text-to-World

Have you seen the Toll House brand named after Wakefield's cookies? Where else have you seen chocolate chip cookies?

Glossary

ancient – from a long time ago.

cacao – tree that grows seeds from which chocolate is made.

dough – mixture of moist flour that is thick enough to roll.

ingredient – one of the items that make up a mixture.

recipe – directions for making a food dish.

Index

Online Resources

popbooksonline.com

Thanks for reading this Cody Koala book!

Scan this code* and others like it in this book, or visit the website below to make this book pop!

popbooksonline.com/chocolate-chip-cookies

*Scanning QR codes requires a web-enabled smart device with a QR code reader app and a camera.